Contents

Introduction 3

Fact 1: Millennials are now the largest, most diverse generation in the U.S. population. 5

Fact 2: Millennials have been shaped by technology. 7

Fact 3: Millennials value community, family, and creativity in their work. 9

Fact 4: Millennials have invested in human capital more than previous generations. 12

Fact 5: College-going Millennials are more likely to study social science and applied fields. 14

Fact 6: As college enrollments grow, more students rely on loans to pay for post-secondary education. 16

Fact 7: Millennials are more likely to focus exclusively on studies instead of combining school and work. .. 18

Fact 8: As a result of the Affordable Care Act, Millennials are much more likely to have health insurance coverage during their young adult years. 20

Fact 9: Millennials will contend with the effects of starting their careers during a historic downturn for years to come. 23

Fact 10: Investments in human capital are likely to have a substantial payoff for Millennials. 27

Fact 11: Working Millennials are staying with their early-career employers longer. 29

Fact 12: Millennial women have more labor market equality than previous generations 31

Fact 13: Millennials tend to get married later than previous generations. 34

Fact 14: Millennials are less likely to be homeowners than young adults in previous generations. .. 37

Fact 15: College-educated Millennials have moved into urban areas faster than their less educated peers. 42

Conclusion 44

References 46

Introduction

Millennials, the cohort of Americans born between 1980 and the mid-2000s, are the largest generation in the U.S., representing one-third of the total U.S. population in 2013.[1] With the first cohort of Millennials only in their early thirties, most members of this generation are at the beginning of their careers and so will be an important engine of the economy in the decades to come.

The significance of Millennials extends beyond their numbers. This is the first generation to have had access to the Internet during their formative years. Millennials also stand out because they are the most diverse and educated generation to date: 42 percent identify with a race or ethnicity other than non-Hispanic white, around twice the share of the Baby Boomer generation when they were the same age.[2] About 61 percent of adult Millennials have attended college, whereas only 46 percent of the Baby Boomers did so.[3]

Yet perhaps the most important marker for Millennials is that many of them have come of age during a very difficult time in our economy, as the oldest Millennials were just 27 years old when the recession began in December 2007. As unemployment surged from 2007 to 2009, many Millennials struggled to find a hold in the labor market. They made important decisions about their educational and career paths, including whether and where to attend college, during a time of great economic uncertainty. Their early adult lives have been shaped by the experience of establishing their careers at a time when economic opportunities are relatively scarce. Today, although the economy is well into its recovery, the recession still affects lives of Millennials and will likely continue to do so for years to come.

This report takes an early look at this generation's adult lives so far, including how they are faring in the labor market and how they are organizing their personal lives. This generation is marked by transformations at nearly every important milestone: from changes in parenting practices and schooling choices, to the condition of the U.S. economy they entered, to their own choices about home and family. However, in many cases, Millennials are simply following the patterns of change that began generations ago.

Millennials are also the generation that will shape our economy for decades to come, and no one understands that more that the President. It's why he has put in place policies to address the various challenges their generation faces. This includes policies such as: making student loan payments more affordable; promoting digital literacy and innovation; pushing for equal pay and paycheck fairness; supporting investments and policies that create better-paying jobs; connecting more Americans to job training and skills programs that prepare them for in-demand jobs; supporting access to credit for those who want to buy a home; and increasing access to affordable health care. And it's why the

---

[1] Census Bureau. There is no strong consensus about how to define Millennials, though several sources attribute the word to historians Neil Howe and William Strauss, who outlined a theory of social generations in American history.
[2] Decennial Census and American Community Survey. Data for Millennials are for those 15 to 34 years old in 2012. Baby Boomers comparisons are for when they were 15 to 34 as surveyed in 1980.
[3] Decennial Census and American Community Survey. Data for Millennials are for those 18 to 34 years old in 2012. Baby Boomers comparisons are for when they were 18 to 34 as surveyed in 1980.

President will continue to act with Congress and on his own where he can to build on this progress to expand opportunity for Millennials and all Americans.

Fact 1: Millennials are now the largest, most diverse generation in the U.S. population.

Millennials now represent the largest generation in the United States, comprising roughly one-third of the total population in 2013. What's more, the largest Millennial one-year age cohort is now only 23. This means that the Millennial generation will continue to be a sizable part of the population for many years (Figure 1).

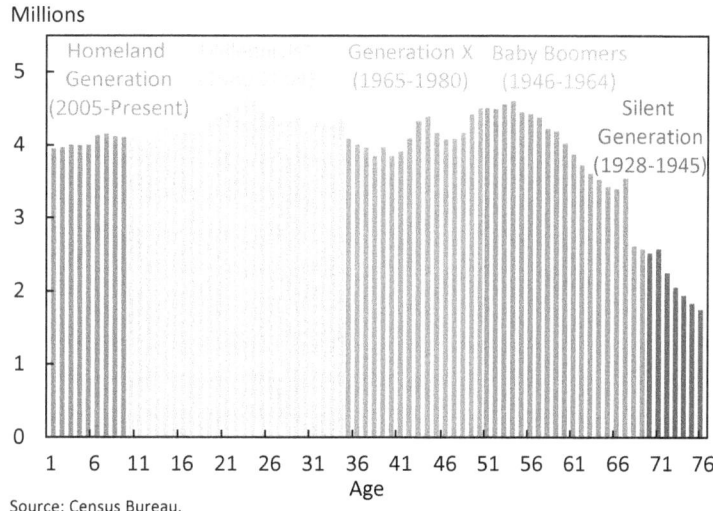

Aside from their numbers, Millennials' diversity sets them apart from other generations. Many Millennials are immigrants or the children of immigrants who arrived in the United States as part of an upsurge in immigration that began in the 1940s. The share of people age 20 to 34 who were born in a foreign country is now around 15 percent – much higher than it was in 1950 and near the peak of almost 20 percent seen in 1910 during the last great wave of immigration to the United States (Figure 2).

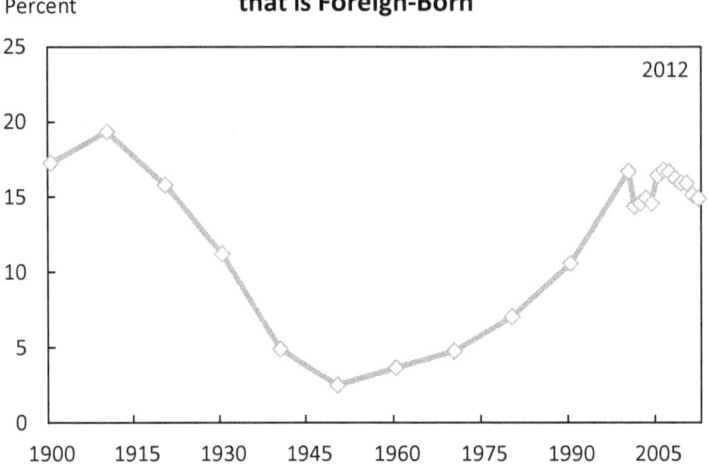

Figure 2: Share of Population Aged 20 to 34 that is Foreign-Born

Source: Decennial Censuses and American Community Survey; CEA calculations.

This influx has contributed to the large size of the Millennial generation and helped make it the most diverse generation in the post-war period. As Figure 3 shows, the share of those age 15 to 34 who identify as non-Hispanic white fell 20 percentage points from 1980 to 2012, while the share reporting Hispanic ancestry tripled.

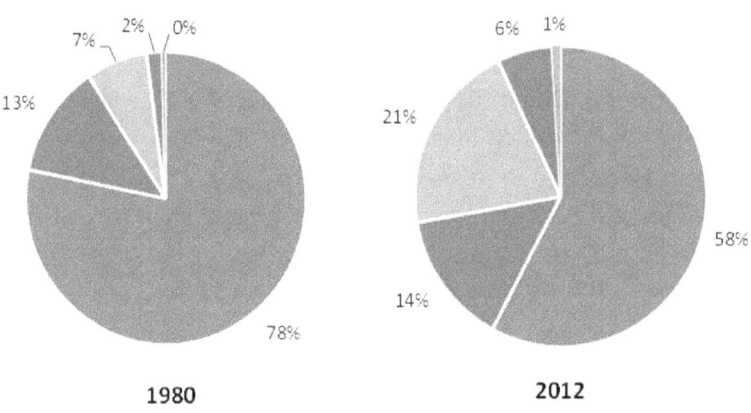

Figure 3: Race and Ethnic Group, 15 to 34 Year-Olds

Source: Census Bureau.

Fact 2: Millennials have been shaped by technology.

The past few decades have witnessed astounding advances in technology and computing. Since personal computers were introduced to schools in the late 1970s, technology companies have innovated at startling speed, often rolling out a groundbreaking new platform or computer model every year. Because much of this period of innovation coincided with Millennials' childhoods, it has shaped the ways that Millennials interact with technology and seems to have affected their expectations for creativity and innovation in their own work lives.

Millennials are more connected to technology than previous generations and a quarter of Millennials believe that their relationship to technology is what makes their generation unique.[4] While all generations have experienced technological advances, the sheer amount of computational power and access to information that Millennials have had at their fingertips since grade-school is unparalleled. Computational processing power has roughly doubled every 2 years, and storage prices continue to drop.[5] In 1980, IBM's first gigabyte hard drive weighed 550 pounds and cost $40,000.[6] Today, consumers have access to 3 terabyte hard drives — 3000 times the size — that weigh under 3 pounds and cost around $100. Under these trends, Millennials have come of age in a world in which the frontiers of technology have appeared unlimited.[7]

At the same time, the costs of creating and distributing all kinds of digital content – from books to music to software – have fallen dramatically.[8] This creates opportunities for this generation to be pioneers in production, as well as consumption, of technology. One study found that more than half of the Millennials surveyed expressed interest in starting a business. And although several Millennials became well-known entrepreneurs in their 20s, this generation is just beginning to reach the peak age for entrepreneurship, which generally occurs in one's 40s or early 50s.[9]

In addition to creating opportunities for entrepreneurship, advances in computer processing power, along with widespread access to cell phones and the Internet, have changed how Millennials communicate and interact with one another. Millennials use social media more frequently and are even more likely to sleep near their cell phone.[10] Three-quarters of Millennials have an account on a social networking site, compared with only half of Generation Xers and less than a third of the Baby Boomers.[11] The impacts of these practices have extended beyond Millennials' peers to their families. For instance, the *Wall Street Journal* reported that this is the first generation to also have tech savvy

---

[4] Pew (2014).
[5] Waldfogel (2013); MIT App Inventor, http://appinventor.mit.edu/explore/
[6] PCWorld, Timeline: 50 Years of Hard Drives, http://www.pcworld.com/article/127105/article.html
[7] Berkeley DataScience, http://datascience.berkeley.edu/moores-law-processing-power/.
[8] Waldfogel (2013); MIT App Inventor, http://appinventor.mit.edu/explore/.
[9] Young Invincibles (2011); Parker (2009).
[10] Taylor and Keeter (2010).
[11] Ibid.

parents, and that some Millennials use texting or online chat to have running conversations with their parents throughout their day.[12]

---

[12] "Mom, Stop Calling, I'll Text You All Day" *Wall Street Journal* July 30, 2013
http://online.wsj.com/news/articles/SB10001424127887324354704578636391784495074

Fact 3: Millennials value community, family, and creativity in their work.

Millennials are not just virtually connected via social networks; they value the role that they play in their communities. For instance, high school seniors today are more likely than previous generations to state that making a contribution to society is very important to them and that they want to be leaders in their communities. This community-mindedness also includes a strong connection to family. Millennials have close relationships with their parents, and as high school students, roughly half say that it is important to them to live close to their friends and family, compared with 29 percent of Baby Boomers and 40 percent of Generation Xers.[13]

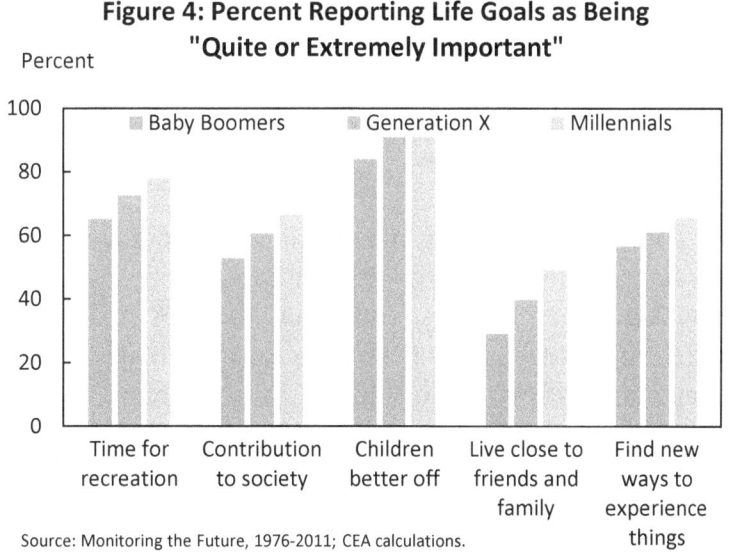

Source: Monitoring the Future, 1976-2011; CEA calculations.

A 1997 Gallup survey found that 9 in 10 children (a population comprised entirely of Millennials that year) reported high levels of closeness with their parents and were personally happy with that relationship.[14] Their tight relationship with their parents extends to work, where some companies report establishing relationships with parents of their Millennial employees.[15] The Millennials' close relationships with their parents might be related to the greater time they spent with their parents growing up. According to Pew (2014), hours spent parenting have increased for both fathers and mothers, tripling for fathers since 1985 and increasing by 60 percent for mothers, as shown in Table 2.[16] Ramey and Ramey (2010) show that these increases have been particularly pronounced among college-educated parents, with college-educated mothers increasing their childcare time since the mid-1990s by over 9 hours per week, while less educated mothers increased their childcare time by only over 4 hours per week.[17]

---

[13] Monitoring the Future (1976-2011).
[14] Howe and Strauss (2000).
[15] Harvard Business Review http://blogs.hbr.org/2014/04/do-millennials-really-want-their-bosses-to-call-their-parents/
[16] Pew (2014).
[17] Ramey and Ramey (2010).

Table 1		
Average Number of Hours		
Year	Fathers	Mothers
1965	2.5	10.2
1975	2.6	8.6
1985	2.6	8.4
1995	4.2	9.6
2000	6.8	12.6
2005	6.8	13.6
2010	7.3	13.5
2011	7.3	13.5

Source: American Time Use, Pew Research Center analysis, http://www.pewresearch.org/data-trend/society-and-demographics/parental-time-use/

When it comes to work, Millennials are mostly similar to previous generations: they want to be successful, and they want the type of prosperity that means that their children will be better off. They are somewhat more likely than previous generations to report that they consider creativity to be a very important job feature. Perhaps this is no surprise for a highly-connected generation for whom technology was a key part of their upbringing. On the other hand, they are less likely to report that having an interesting job, or one where they can see results or have advancement opportunities, is very important.

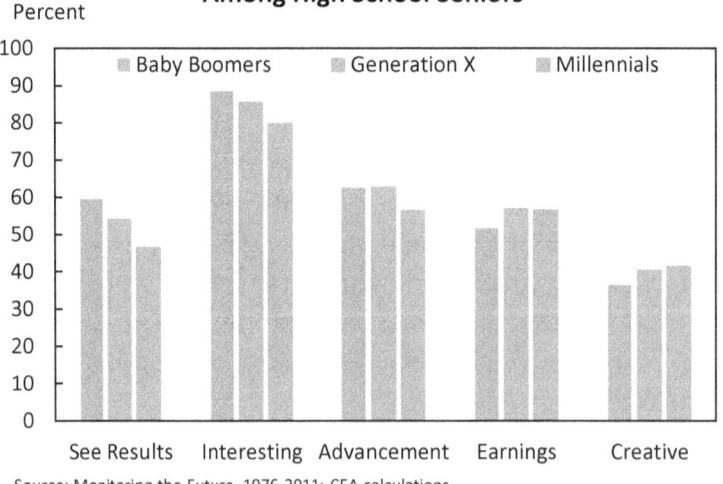

Figure 5: "Very Important" Job Characteristics Among High School Seniors

Source: Monitoring the Future, 1976-2011; CEA calculations.

While many Millennials report that earnings are very important to them in a job, breaking the data down by gender reveals that this change is driven primarily by young women. Each cohort of young women is more likely than the last to name earnings as a key job feature, while the importance of earnings has been stable for men. The result is that Millennial women have aspirations that are similar to their male peers.

In sum, quality of life appears to be a focus of this generation: Millennials value staying close to family and friends, having free time for recreation, and working in creative jobs. However, they also want to make a positive social impact on their own children and communities, as well as on society as a whole.

Fact 4: Millennials have invested in human capital more than previous generations.

More Millennials have a college degree than any other generation of young adults. In 2013, 47 percent of 25 to 34 year-olds received a postsecondary degree (associates, bachelor's, or graduate degree) and an additional 18 percent had completed some postsecondary education, as Figure 6 shows. Also, because the rate of young workers with some post-secondary education but no degree has been flat while the share with a degree has risen, more students are completing the degrees they start after high school.

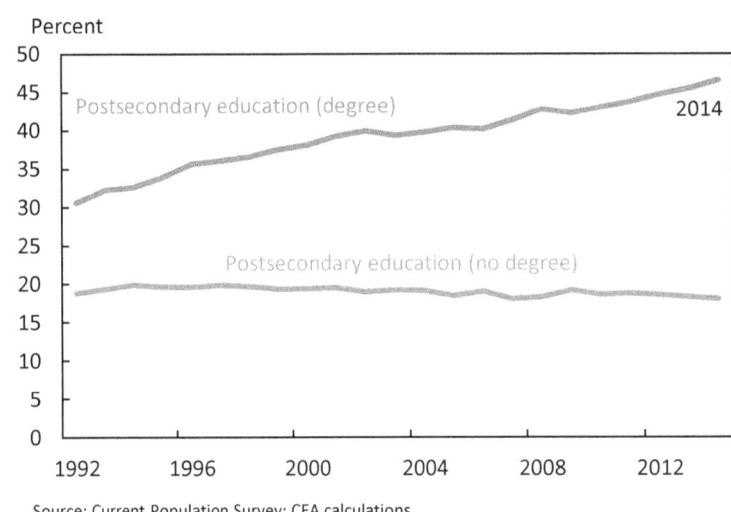

Figure 6: People Ages 25 to 34 By Educational Attainment,

Source: Current Population Survey; CEA calculations.

Increasing college enrollment is in part a response to decades of rising returns to education for workers and heightened income inequality between the college-educated and the less-educated. Millennials' commitment to higher education is therefore a rational response to a labor market that confers large rewards on more educated workers. Moreover, during recessions, young people tend to enroll in school in greater numbers and also tend to stay in school longer.[18] This cyclical pattern reflects both a lower opportunity cost of schooling, as well as a stronger incentive to make one's skills competitive in a tough job market.

Millennials are also more likely to attend graduate school than previous generations. Among 18 to 34 year-olds, college enrollment stood at 19 percent in 2010, up from 15 percent in 1995. Graduate school enrollment for the same age group has increased at an even faster rate, jumping from 2.8 percent in 1995 to 3.8 percent in 2010 – a 35 percent increase.

With so many Millennials enrolling in college, there has been an unprecedented expansion of higher education to lower-income and underrepresented minority students. Figure 7 shows that enrollment

---

[18] Card and Lemieux (2000); Long (2013). However, note that Oreopoulos, von Wachter and Heisz (2012) find that unemployment rates have insignificant impacts on college duration.

of all students in degree-granting institutions has increased over time, but more recent gains have been greatest among black and Hispanic students. Since 1995, enrollment for blacks ages 18 to 24 increased 9 percentage points and enrollment for Hispanics ages 18 to 24 increased 17 percentage points. These represent larger increases, in percentage terms, for blacks and Hispanics than for whites. Research has also found that enrollment of students from low-income families is higher among Millennials than previous generations.[19]

Figure 7: Enrollment rates of 18 to 24 year-olds in degree-granting institutions

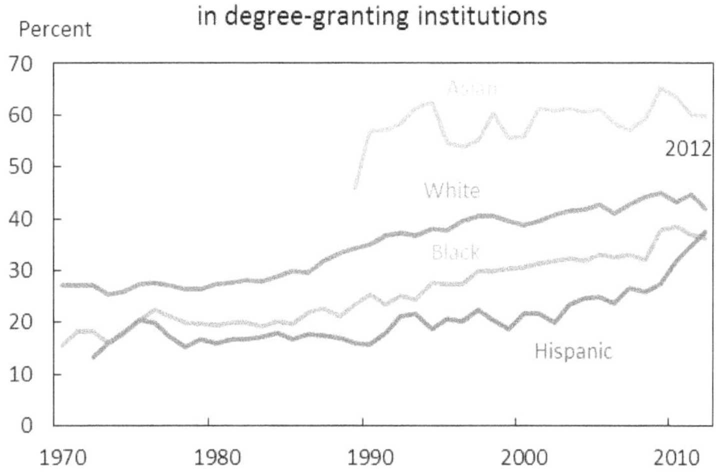

Source: National Center for Education Statistics; CEA calculations.

---

[19] Bailey and Dynarski (2011).

Fact 5: College-going Millennials are more likely to study social science and applied fields.

Millennials are more likely to study social science or applied fields—like communications, criminal justice, and library science—that do not fit into traditional liberal arts curricula, but correspond more directly to specific careers (Figure 8).

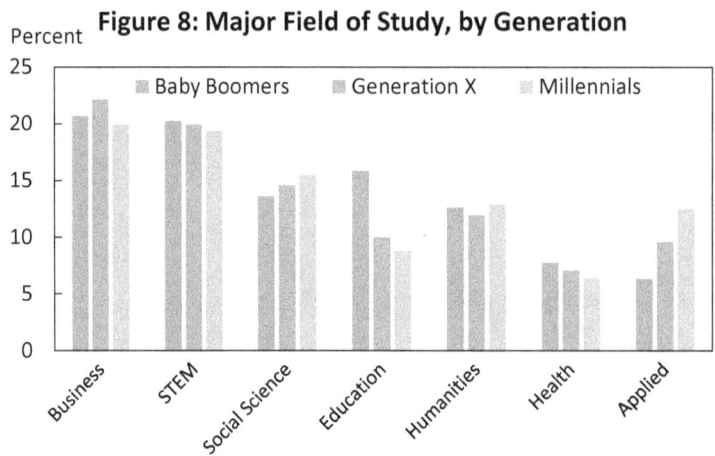

Source: American Community Survey, 2009-2012; CEA calculations.
Note: Millennials: born 1980 or later, Gen X: born 1965-79, Baby Boomers: born 1946-64. The "applied" category includes communications, library science, criminial justice, culinary arts, and similar fields.

There has also been a significant decline in the share of students majoring in education since Baby Boomers were in college, as shown in Figure 8. This decrease is mostly explained by a sharp move away from education degrees among female college students. About 35 percent of women graduating from college in the early 1970s earned a degree in an education-related field, but only about 12 percent did in 2011. Business degrees have become more popular among women over the same period, increasing from 9 percent of the class of 1970 to 16 percent of the class of 2011, after peaking in the mid-1980s for both men and women.

Millennials are also somewhat less likely than previous generations to major in fields like business and health (which includes pre-med and nursing). The share of Millennials studying STEM fields is slightly lower than that of past generations; however, the absolute number of majors in these fields has increased over time as college enrollment has expanded, just not as fast as the number of students in other majors.[20]

Perhaps surprisingly for a technologically-connected generation, the share of Millennials choosing computer and information science majors has fallen over time, and this decline has been most pronounced among women. In 1987, 2.9 percent of women graduating with a bachelor's degree received a degree in computer and information science, and women comprised 36 percent of all computer science graduates. In contrast, in the class of 2011, only 1.1 percent of women graduated

---

[20] Digest of Education Statistics..

with computer science degrees, and women comprised only 18 percent of all computer science graduates. Over the same period, the share of men graduating with such degrees fell only slightly, from 5.7 percent to 5.4 percent. This trend in computer science stands in stark contrast with other highly-compensated fields, such as medicine, dentistry, and law, where women's participation has increased over this period.[21]

---

[21] CEA (2014b).

Fact 6: As college enrollments grow, more students rely on loans to pay for post-secondary education.

Total student outstanding loan debt surpassed $1 trillion by the end of the second quarter of 2014, making it the second largest category of household debt. In part, this increase in the aggregate level of outstanding student debt is due to greater enrollment among Millennials and to the changing composition of students, including a larger share of students from lower-income families who need to take out more loans, as discussed in Fact 4. Other contributing factors include: rising tuition as state governments have cut funding; parents' impaired ability to use the equity in their homes to offset some portion of their children's college costs; and the fact that students are taking longer to repay their loans. Consistent with these factors, average real per borrower debt increased from $24,000 in 2004 to $30,000 in 2012.[22] Since 2012, total originations have fallen, and since 2010, originations per borrower have fallen; however, the fraction of students borrowing remains high from a longer-term perspective. Around half of students borrowed student loans during the 2013-14 school year, up from around 30 percent in the mid-1990s.[23]

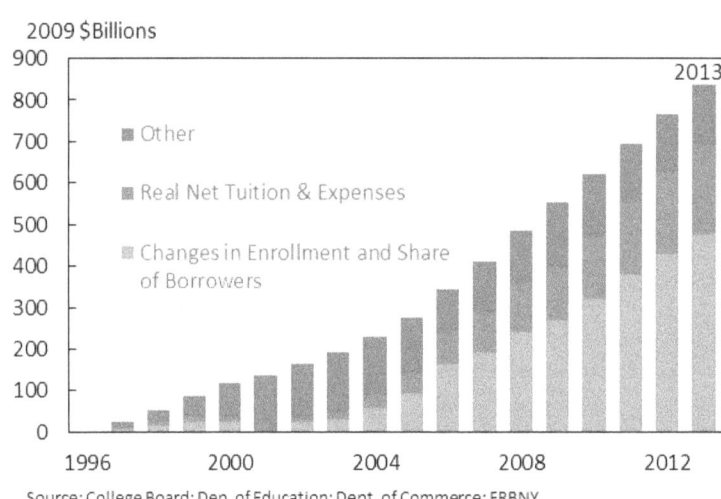

Figure 9: Sources of Change in Student Loan Debt

Source: College Board; Dep. of Education; Dept. of Commerce; FRBNY.

With the gap in earnings between college- and high school-educated workers both large and growing, college-educated Millennials are more likely to earn higher wages and be employed than those without a college degree. A four-year degree yields approximately $570,000 more in lifetime earnings than a high school diploma alone, while a two-year degree yields $170,000 more.[24] Importantly, research finds that the earnings gains from attending college are broad-based, as both lower-skilled students attending basic college programs and higher-skilled students attending elite colleges stand to benefit.[25]

---

[22] National Postsecondary Student Aid Study.
[23] Goldman Sachs (2014).
[24] U.S. Treasury (2014).
[25] See, e.g. Zimmerman (2014) for estimates on low-skilled youth, and Hoekstra (2009) for estimates on more skilled students.

However, one concern with rising average student debt levels is that a non-trivial minority of borrowers might face financial difficulties managing and paying down their debt. Recent increases in the prevalence of delinquent student loans point to some of the challenges that borrowers face.[26] In addition, the defaults appear to be concentrated among borrowers who do not graduate from a four-year institution and those attending for-profit institutions. Since borrowers may also receive lower returns to their education from such institutions, the burden of paying back their loans may present an even greater financial challenge.[27]

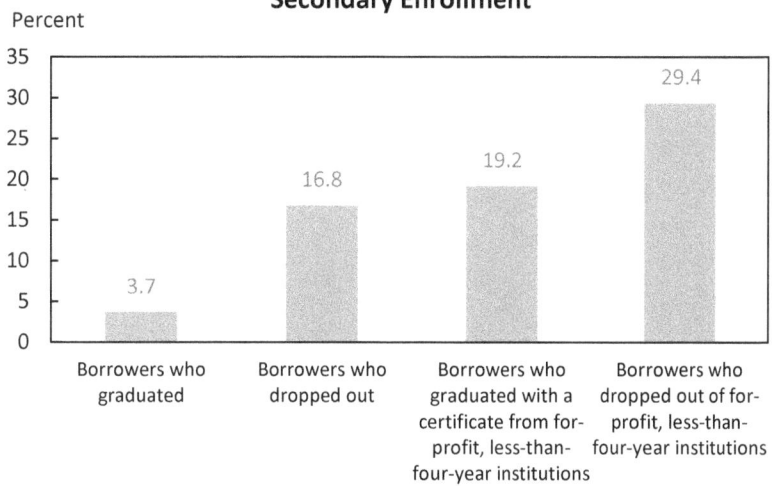

Figure 10: Percentage of Borrowers Who Defaulted on Their Loans up to Six Years after Initial Post-Secondary Enrollment

Source: Beginning Postsecondary Students, BPS: 2004/2009; CEA calculations.

---

[26] Federal Reserve Bank of New York (2014).
[27] Deming, et al. (2014).

Fact 7: Millennials are more likely to focus exclusively on studies instead of combining school and work.

With college enrollments at historic highs there has been a corresponding decline in labor market participation among 16 to 24 year-olds. As Figure 11 shows, about 90 percent of young adults are either enrolled in school or participating in the labor market. This share has been flat since the late 1980s, while labor market participation itself has been declining for this group since the late 1970s. Much of the decline in participation has occurred among students, as students have become more likely to focus on school alone rather than combining school and work.

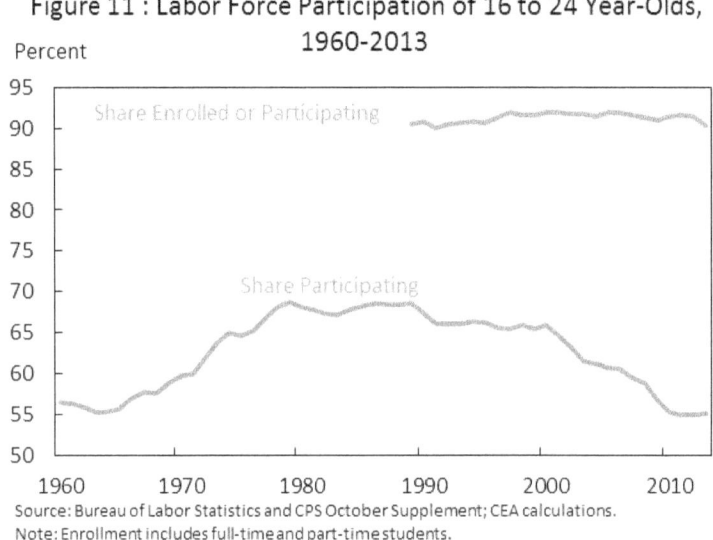

Figure 11 : Labor Force Participation of 16 to 24 Year-Olds, 1960-2013

Source: Bureau of Labor Statistics and CPS October Supplement; CEA calculations.
Note: Enrollment includes full-time and part-time students.

Millennials, in particular, have been less likely to work while enrolled in high school. Since 2000, labor force participation rates among high school and college students have fallen more sharply than those who are not enrolled, as shown in Figure 12.[28] The result is that more students are focused exclusively on their studies during school years. On the other hand, labor force participation has been relatively stable for 18 to 24 year-olds who are not in school. Although participation has also declined somewhat for very young non-enrolled individuals ages 16 to 18, this group is very small and shrinking over time as fewer students are dropping out of high school.

---

[28] Scott-Clayton (2012) also finds that college students have become less likely to work for pay while enrolled over this period.

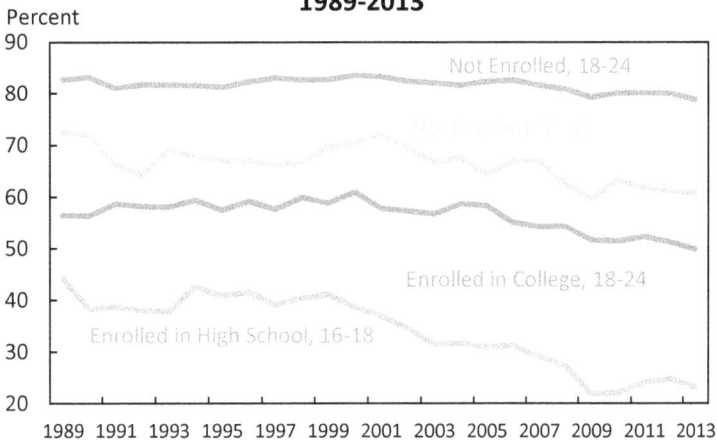

Figure 12: Labor Force Participation by Enrollment Status, 1989-2013

Source: Current Population Survey; CEA calculations.
Note: Enrollment includes full-time and part-time students.

Focusing exclusively on school enables students to invest more time building skills that will be highly rewarded in the labor market later on. Moreover, research suggests that the returns to working during the school year, particularly while in high school, have declined over time.[29] These trends in participation make economic sense. As Millennials enter the labor market after finishing school, these investments can also start to pay off for the economy as a whole.

---

[29] Baum and Ruhm (2014).

Fact 8: As a result of the Affordable Care Act, Millennials are much more likely to have health insurance coverage during their young adult years.

As a result of the Affordable Care Act, Millennials have much better health insurance options during their young adult years than past generations. Since September 2010, young adults have generally been eligible to remain on a parent's health insurance policy until they turn 26. Previously, young adults frequently lost access to a parent's plan when they turned 19 or graduated from college. In addition, as of the beginning of 2014, many young adults newly qualify for tax credits to purchase health insurance coverage through the Health Insurance Marketplaces or Medicaid in States that have accepted Federal funding to expand their Medicaid programs.

From the time the Affordable Care Act's dependent coverage provision took effect in 2010 through the first quarter of 2014, the uninsurance rate among individuals ages 19 to 25 fell by 13.2 percentage points, a 40 percent decline.[30] In the first quarter of 2014, the share of young adults without health insurance coverage was 20.9 percent, the lowest young adult uninsured rate recorded since the National Health Interview Survey began using its current design in 1997.[31] Other analyses using private survey data show that overall insurance coverage continued to expand during the second quarter of 2014, so these estimated gains are likely to grow in the coming months. Moreover, analysts predict that coverage will continue to expand in the years ahead.[32]

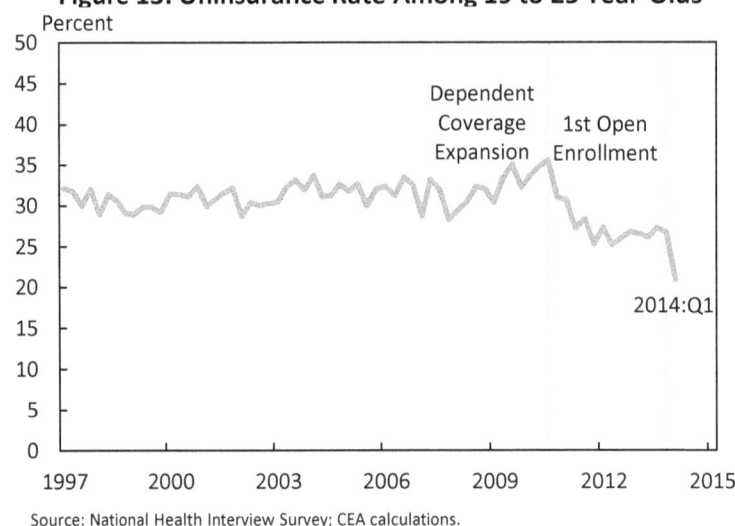

Source: National Health Interview Survey; CEA calculations.

Having health insurance has been shown to improve access to health care, health outcomes, and financial security.[33] Research focused on the Affordable Care Act's dependent coverage expansion has

---

[30] This change is measured relative to the average uninsurance rate from 2009:Q4-2010:Q3. The dependent coverage provision took effect on September 23, 2010, a week before the end of 2010:Q3.
[31] Cohen and Martinez (2014).
[32] Sommers et al. (2014); Long et al. (2014); CBO (2014); Sisko et al. (2014).
[33] CEA (2014a).

found evidence for similar effects. Researchers have found that in tandem with the sharp increase in insurance coverage following the law's enactment, young adults became less likely to delay or entirely forgo care due to cost and markedly less likely to face large out-of-pocket medical expenditures.[34] Several studies have also concluded that these newly-insured young adults are more likely receive several types of inpatient and outpatient care, while another found that they are more likely to report being in excellent health.[35]

Greater access to health insurance coverage outside the workplace during young adulthood may also generate important labor market benefits by allowing workers to obtain additional schooling or choose the jobs that best match their career goals. Research examining the Affordable Care Act's dependent coverage expansion has documented increased school enrollment among young adults, and earlier research examining similar state laws found significant gains in ultimate educational attainment as well as higher wages later in life.[36] Other research has similarly found that the Affordable Care Act's dependent coverage expansion reduced employment lock and increased labor market flexibility, allowing workers to change jobs without the fear of losing health insurance.[37]

Millennials are also poised to benefit from another important development in our nation's health care system: the striking slowdown in the growth of health care costs. From the time the oldest Millennials were born through when they turned age 25 in 2005, private employers' costs for health benefits grew at an average annual rate of 5.4 percent, adjusted for inflation. But in recent years, the growth of real health benefit costs has fallen dramatically, averaging just 1.1 percent over the last two years, about 80 percent lower than the prior average (see Figure 14). Economic theory and empirical evidence demonstrate that higher benefit costs are ultimately borne by workers in the form of lower wages and salaries.[38] As a result, if the dramatic slowdown in the growth of health benefit costs persists in the years ahead, it will help drive faster growth in wages and salaries for Millennials relative to their predecessors.

_____

[34] Sommers et al. (2013). Blum (2012). Chua and Sommers (2013).
[35] Antwi, Moriya, and Simon (2014); Blum (2012); Saloner (2014); Chua and Sommers (2014).
[36] Depew (2012); Dillender (2014).
[37] Hulbert (2012). Antwi, Moriya, and Simon (2013).
[38] Summers (1989); Gruber and Krueger (1991); Gruber (1994); Baicker and Chandra (2006).

Figure 14: Growth in Employer Health Benefit Costs, 1981-2014

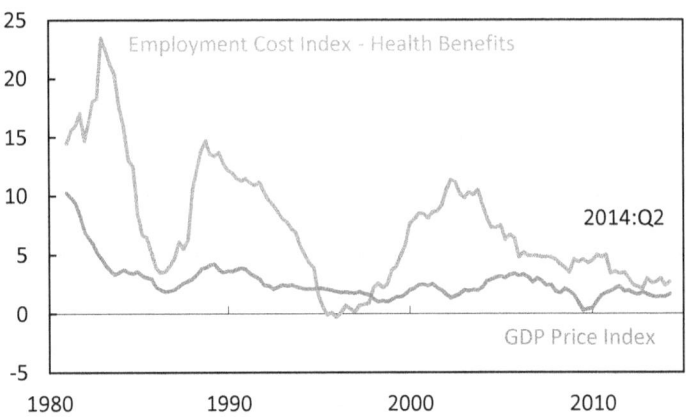

Source: Bureau of Labor Statistics, Bureau of Economic Analysis; CEA calculations.

Fact 9: Millennials will contend with the effects of starting their careers during a historic downturn for years to come.

Millennials are currently about a third of the labor force and, as a generation, they have faced substantial challenges in entering the workforce during the most pronounced downturn since the Great Recession. The overall unemployment rate for young workers between ages 18 to 34 peaked at over 13 percent in 2010, on a seasonally-adjusted basis. Since then it has come down 4.7 percentage points to 8.6 percent in September 2014. While it remains elevated, the labor market recovery and decline in the unemployment rate has recently been faster than any time since the early 1980s. Between June 2013 and June 2014, the unemployment rate of Millennials declined by 1.8 percentage points, the largest reduction in unemployment for this age group also since the early-1980s. During this period of rapid decline in the unemployment rate, the number of employed Millennials increased by 990,000, a noticeable acceleration from the 786,000 Millennials that found work during the year-earlier period.

Examining the twelve month averages of various measures of unemployment, allows us to look at how much different indicators of unemployment have recovered for this age group compared to their prerecession averages. The 12-month average of the unemployment rate as of August 2014 for Millennials is roughly three-quarters of the way back to its pre-recession average, broadly in line with the extent of recovery for other groups. [39] The recent improvement in labor market conditions for Millennials broadly mirrors that of the broader population, as do the outstanding challenges. The fraction of Millennials unemployed for less than 26 weeks has recovered more than the fraction of long-term unemployed, just as is the case for the population as a whole. Long-term unemployment remains a challenge for Millennials and for the country in general, as we work to get more of the long-term unemployed back into employment.

---

[39] Because seasonally adjusted data for this age group is not available, we examine 12-month averages. Since the labor market continued to improve over the past 12 months, these averages will understate the extent of recovery. Current Population Survey Microdata were only available through August 2014 at the time this report was published.

Figure 15: Labor Market Indicators in the Recession for Millennials
All Data as of August 2014

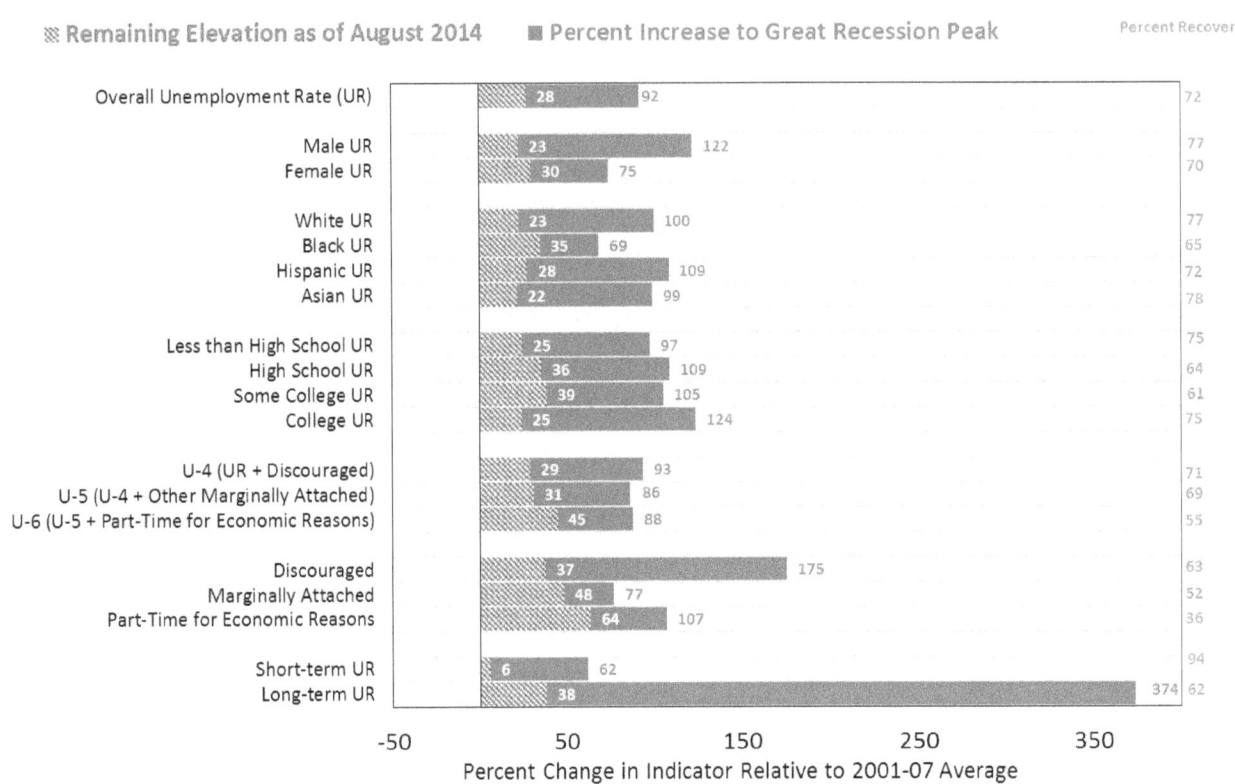

Source: Current Population Survey, January 2001-August 2014; CEA calculations.
Note: Data for August 2014 are a 12-month average over September 2013 to August 2014, for ages 18 to 34 and are not seasonally adjusted.

Other indicators tell a similar story—while Millennials have made a substantial labor market recovery, that recovery is not complete and is slightly lagging that of other age groups, consistent with prior recessions. Broader measures of joblessness also indicate that the recovery is making progress. For example, measures of unemployment that account for people who are discouraged from looking for work or are only available for work under certain conditions were roughly 70 percent back as of the 12-month average ending in August 2014 to their pre-recession average, while those that include people who are working part-time, but would prefer full-time hours were 55 percent recovered.

The unemployment rate has recovered similarly among Millennials regardless of education, however, this similarity masks big differences in the levels of unemployment by education. The unemployment rate of 25-34 year old Millennials with a college degree was 3.7 percent in 2013, compared to 13.5 percent among those less than a high school education.

The pace of the recovery for younger age groups is in line with the pattern we typically see after a recession, as shown in Figure 16 yet more work remains to be done to ensure a full recovery. Younger workers have less experience and more tenuous connections to employers than older workers, so they are often laid off in greater numbers and have to compete against more experienced workers for new jobs once recovery begins. They therefore tend to be among the last groups to recover fully from a recession.

Figure 16: Unemployment Rate of Workers Ages 16 to 24 During Recoveries

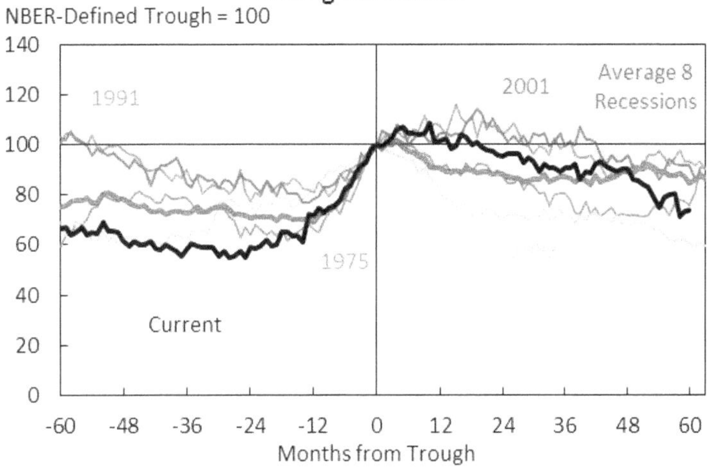

Source: Bureau of Labor Statistics; CEA calculations.

The Great Recession likely will have important implications for Millennials' future labor force outcomes, since research finds that macroeconomic conditions in childhood and young adulthood are important determinants of future earnings and financial behavior. Early career economic conditions have large and lasting impacts on lifetime wages, particularly for college graduates. Research shows that entering the labor market during a recession can result in substantial earnings losses that persist for more than a decade, with negative effects lasting longer for college graduates.[40] Workers who start their careers in a recession earn 2.5 to 9 percent less per year than those who do not for at least 15 years after starting a career. Research further suggests that one reason for these lower earnings is that new entrants take jobs that are a worse fit for them when they start their careers in a recession.[41]

However, research also shows that perhaps the single most important determinant of a person's income is their level of education. And as the most educated generation in history, this will tend to boost earnings for Millennials over the course of their lifetimes—and help to offset any longer-term harms from the Great Recession.

Millennials themselves remain largely optimistic about their ability to move up socioeconomically, with over half agreeing that people like them have a good chance of improving their standard of living. While this number has been trending down in the wake of recent economic turmoil, following a more long-standing decline that began in 2000 (Figure 17), Millennials, like all young people, are more optimistic than older respondents.

---

[40] Kahn (2010); Oreopoulos et al. (2012), Wozniak (2010).

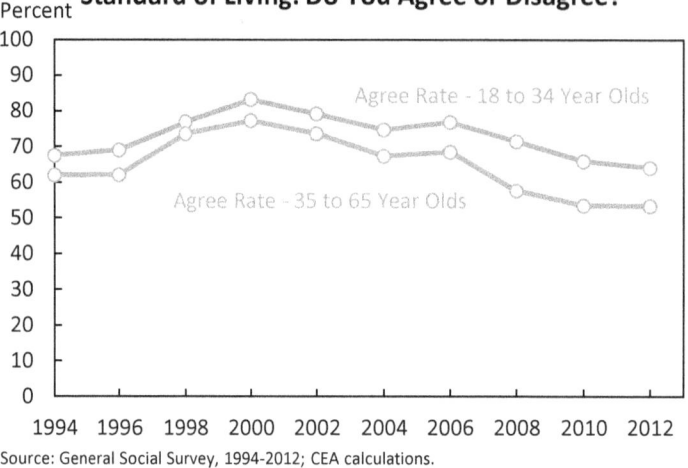

Figure 17: The Way Things are in America, People Like Me and My Family Have a Good Chance of Improving Our Standard of Living: Do You Agree or Disagree?

Source: General Social Survey, 1994-2012; CEA calculations.

Overall, these economic conditions may affect adult financial behavior and beliefs about success and the role of institutions in society. Individuals who experienced the Great Depression invested less and pursued more conservative investing strategies throughout their lives.[42] More recent economic turmoil has bigger impacts on behavior and that these impacts are most pronounced for younger savers. This suggests that the Great Recession will impact early savings and investment behavior among Millennials, but at this point, it is still too soon to know how large these impacts will be.

---

[42] Malmendier and Nagel (2011).

Fact 10: Investments in human capital are likely to have a substantial payoff for Millennials.

Recent college graduates continue to out-earn individuals with only a high school diploma, a gap that has been increasing over time. The college premium, the difference between median earnings for college versus high school graduates, increased from 60 percent in 2004 to roughly 70 percent in 2013. Holding a college degree (associates or bachelor's) results in a much lower probability of having earnings in the lowest income tax bracket—16 to 28 percent for college degree holders versus 37 to 41 percent for those with no college degree (Figure 18). Bachelor's degree holders are also 6 times more likely to have earnings in the top income tax bracket than those with only a high school degree. In addition to earning higher wages on average, individuals with a college degree are less likely to be unemployed. As of September 2014, the unemployment rate for those with a bachelor's degree is around 3 percent, compared with over 5 percent for high school graduates.

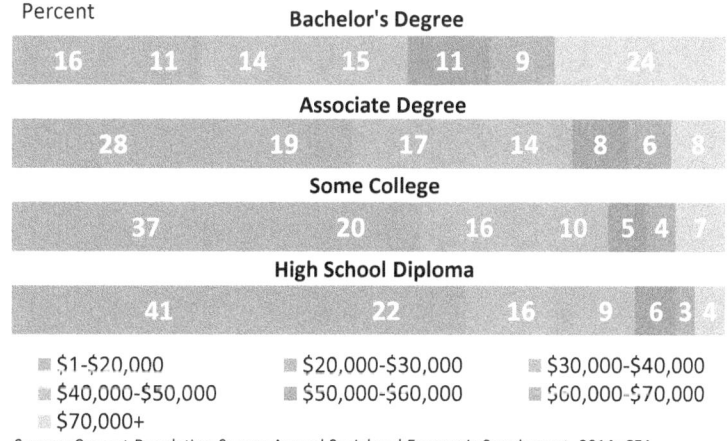

Returns to education are 5 to 10 percent per year of schooling, with most estimates in the 7 to 10 percent range.[43] The gains from a college education are high, both for lower-skilled students attending basic college programs and for stronger students attending selective colleges.[44] Median real hourly wages for 21 to 25 year-old college graduates are even higher than median real hourly wages for 26 to 34 year-old non-college graduates, who have had more time in the labor market. College therefore remains a strong investment for most students—and will raise income levels for Millenials for decades to come well above where they would have been without those investments.

---

[43] Psacharopoulos and Patrinos (2004); Card (1999).
[44] See, e.g. Zimmerman (2014) for estimates on low-skilled youth, and Hoekstra (2009) for estimates on more able students.

While education remains a good investment, Millennials still face challenges associated with several decades of slow wage growth – compounded by the Great Recession. As a result Millennials have seen slower wage growth than earlier generations of young adults. The typical employed college graduate who entered the market in the mid- to late-1990s saw his or her wages increase by around 50 percent between the ages of 23 and 28. This indicator of wage growth for young workers declined to 24 percent in 2001 and 2002, then recovered somewhat to exceed 30 percent before falling again to under 25 percent for college graduates who entered the labor market at the start of the Great Recession.

Figure 19: Wage Growth for College-Educated Workers Between Ages 23 and 28, by Cohort

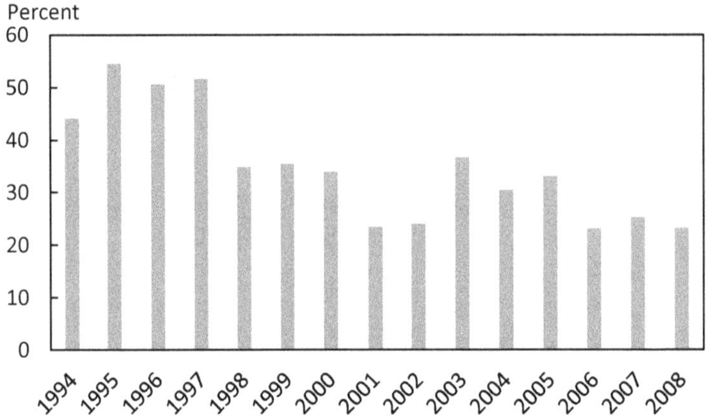

Source: Current Population Survey, 1994-2008; CEA calculations.
Note: Cohorts are grouped by the year in which individuals turned 23.

Fact 11: Working Millennials are staying with their early-career employers longer.

Millennials are sometimes characterized as lacking attachment or loyalty to their employers, but in fact, as Figure 20 shows, contrary to popular perceptions Millennials actually stay with their employers longer than Generation X workers did at the same ages. This reflects the fact that Millennials face a labor market characterized by longer job tenure, fewer employer switches and other types of career transitions, and lower overall fluidity in the labor market.[45] Figure 20 shows that Millennials are less likely to have been with their employer for less than a year than Generation X workers were at the same age, and they are more likely to have been with their employer for a fairly long period like 3 to 6 years.[46]

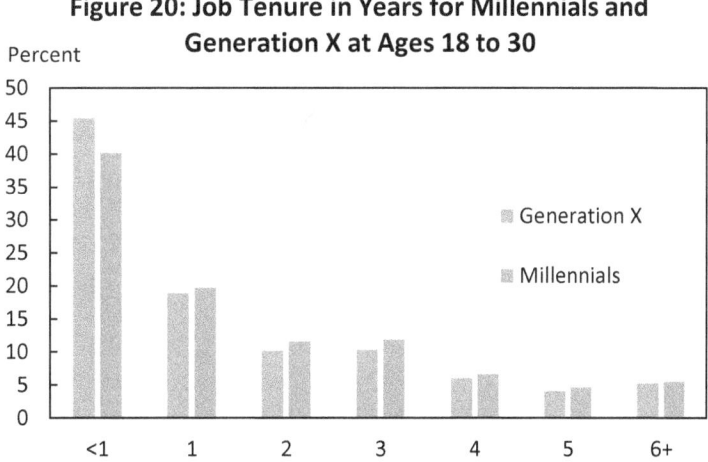

Sources: Current Population Survey Job Tenure Supplement, 1996-2010; CEA calculations.
Note: Data for Generation X (born 1965-1979) reweighted to match age distribution of Millennials (born 1980 or later).

Young workers spending more years with their employers has important advantages in terms of job security, the benefits of learning on the job, and the additional productivity associated with reduced turnover. To the degree that the increase in tenure reflects improved job matches it represents a favorable development. But longer tenures come with potential trade-offs.. Switching jobs has historically been a major source of wage growth for young workers, and longer spells with the same employer raises concerns that reduced fluidity of labor markets may be curtailing wage growth, particularly for young workers.[47]

The flip side of increased job tenure across the economy may be the fact that when people become unemployed they stay unemployed for longer. This has been reflected in the unusually large rise in long-term unemployment in the wake of the recession, a fact that has also affected young workers as

---

[45] Davis and Haltiwanger (2014); Hyatt and Spletzer (2013).
[46] Based on CEA regression analysis when controlling for age and demographic characteristics like educational attainment, gender, and race and ethnicity. These are statistically significant differences. Microdata for this analysis are currently only available through 2010.
[47] Topel and Ward (1992).

shown in Figure 21. Moreover, long-term unemployment appears to have trended up in recent decades. This means some young workers will face longer spells of unemployment in their early years than did past cohorts, which may reduce earnings for affected workers as building employment experience takes more time. Again, education can play a critical role because the increased educational attainment of Millenials will tend to go in the opposite direction, reducing unemployment and helping them build job experience over time.

Figure 21: Prevalence of Long-Term Unemployment Among Ages 20 to 34

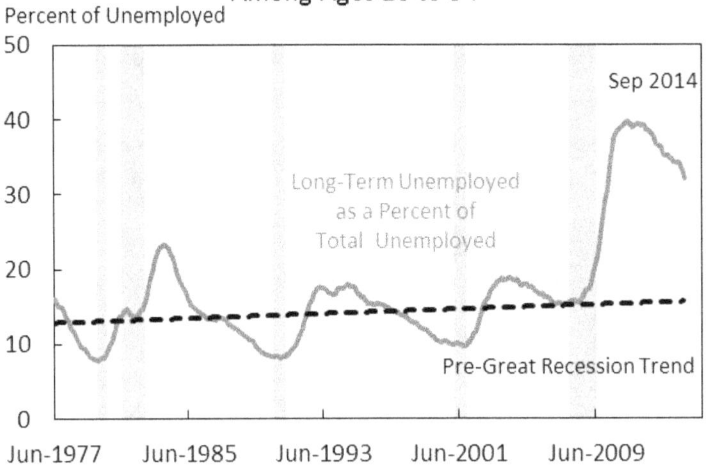

Source: Bureau of Labor Statistics; CEA calculations.

Fact 12: Millennial women have more labor market equality than previous generations

Millennials are not only the most highly educated U.S. generation to date, but a larger share of that increase has come from the educational attainment of women. Millennial women are attending college and attaining degrees in greater numbers than in the past. Women have closed an educational attainment gap with men that dates back to World War II, as shown in Figure 22.[48] In fact, starting in the late 1990s, just as the first Millennial cohorts were completing high school, women began to outpace men in completion of both four-year college degrees and post-college educational attainment.

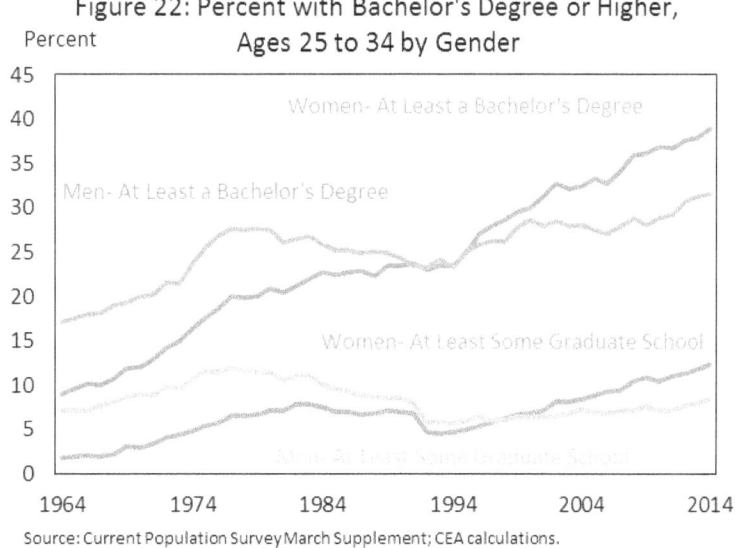

That Millennial women on average exceed Millennial men in terms of educational attainment means that they account for an increasingly large share of our skilled workforce and enter the labor force with early career earnings and employment rates that are considerably closer to their male peers than past generations. Figure 23 shows that hourly wages, earnings, labor force participation, and employment for young women have risen relative to those for young men in every decade since 1980.

---

[48] Goldin, Katz and Kuziemko (2006)..

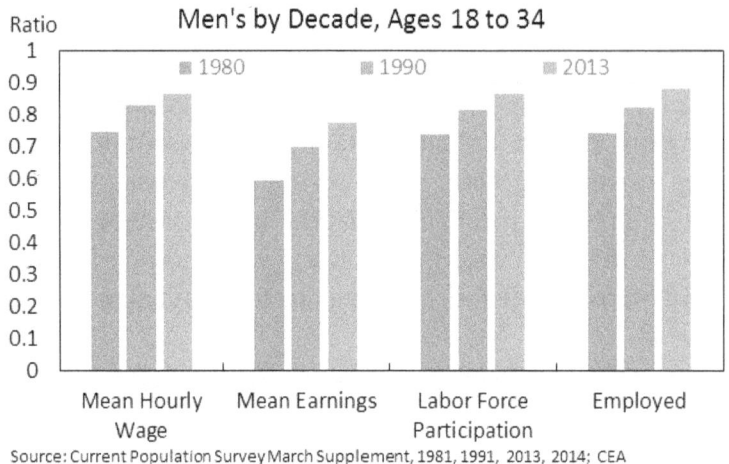

Figure 23: Ratio of Women's Labor Market Outcomes to Men's by Decade, Ages 18 to 34

Source: Current Population Survey March Supplement, 1981, 1991, 2013, 2014; CEA calculations.
Note: Earnings ratio is the ratio of mean wage and salary income of all workers. Hourly wage

Millennial women are making a strong start in the labor market because they are reaping the benefits of their greater investments in education, but Millennial women are not the only beneficiaries of their investments in education and hard work. Their higher earnings translate into greater household income for their families. This is critical to the one in four Millennial households with children where the mother is the sole breadwinner, an arrangement that is more common for Millennials, as shown in Figure 24. Women's incomes are essential to supporting the well-being of even more families since all parents work in roughly 70 percent of Millennial households with children.[49]

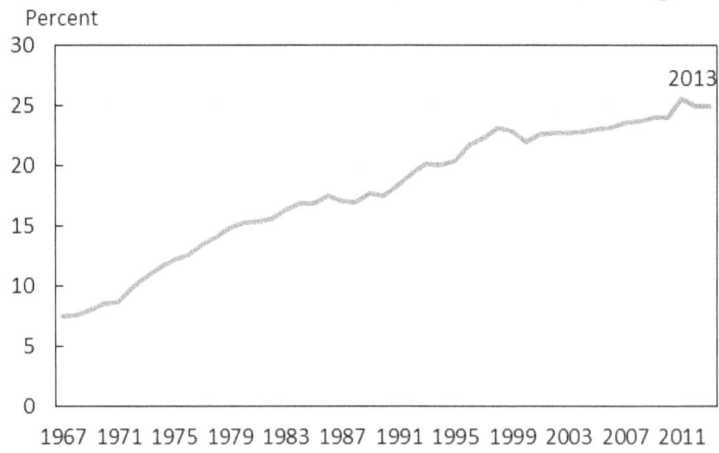

Figure 24: Share of Households with a Parent Age 22 to 34 with Children in Which Only the Mother is Working

Source: Current Population Survey March Supplement; CEA calculations.

The benefits to working for Millennial women are greater, and their incomes are more important to their families, than for past generations of American women. Young men and women recognize the

---

[49] Current Population Survey, March Supplement 2014. CEA calculations.

important role that women's earnings play in the household. Almost all young men and women think that women with school age children should work and more than half think that women should work when they have children younger than school age (Figure 25).[50] However, there is a large gap in the views of men and women. The share of women who think that women should work while they have pre-school aged children has grown rapidly in recent years. Focusing on young women ages 18 to 22 reveals that as of 2002, 82 percent believed that women with young children should work. Men's attitudes have moved less in recent years and remain below that of women, with only roughly 50 percent of men agreeing. The gender disparity may reflect the fact that women recognize how difficult it is for them to reenter the labor force after stepping out for several years. Yet, both men and women, recognize the challenges of balancing work and family obligations, a factor that may influence their preferences about women working with small children.

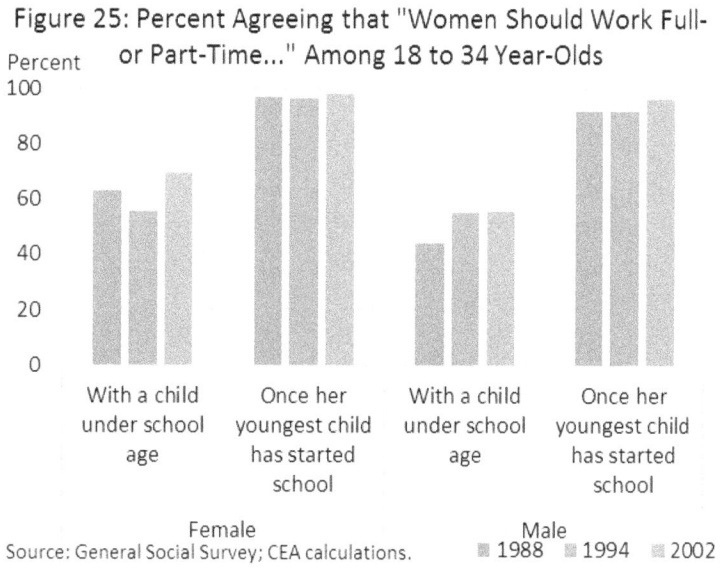

[50] General Social Survey

Fact 13: Millennials tend to get married later than previous generations.

Since 1950, the median age at which both men and women have married has steadily increased. In 1950, men first married at age 22.8 and women at age 20.3; by 2013 the median marriage age increased by more than 6 years for both genders, reaching 29.0 and 26.6 for men and women respectively. As more young adults delay marriage, the fraction of young adults who are currently married has fallen. Millennials have continued on this path and are marrying later, with more of them remaining unmarried in their 20s. In 2013, only 30 percent of 20 to 34 year-olds were married, compared to 77 percent in 1960.[51]

Many factors explain the later marriages including the fact that those with more education (a group whose size has been increasing over time) tend to marry later. However, college-educated Millennials are more likely than the rest of their peers to be married. This reflects a shift in marriage-education patterns: in 1980, those with a college-degree were the least likely to be married. This difference is largely reflective of changes in the marital behavior of women. For much of history, women with college-degrees were the least likely among their peers to ever marry. In more recent decades, college-educated women caught up, largely by marrying at later ages.[52] For instance, among college graduates, 20 percent had not married by age 35 in 2000, yet 43 percent of those married within the next 10 years.[53] The fact that so many now marry later makes it difficult to predict what marriage rates will ultimately look like for this generation.

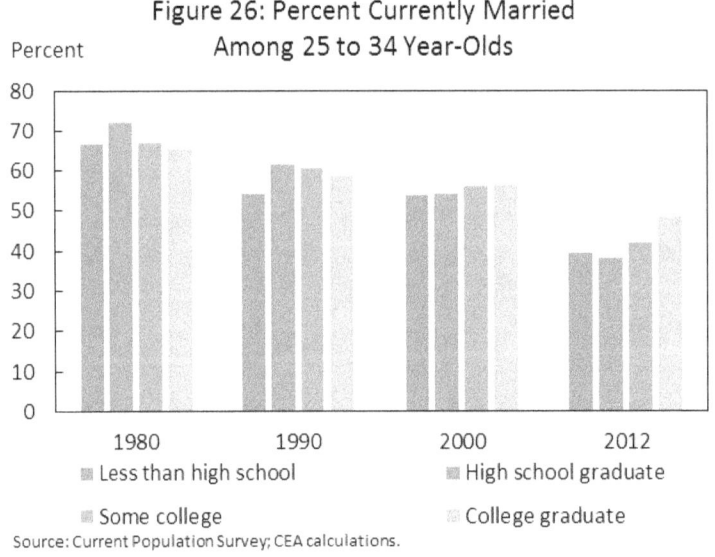

Figure 26: Percent Currently Married Among 25 to 34 Year-Olds
Source: Current Population Survey; CEA calculations.

Although Millennials are delaying marriage, this does not mean that they do not want to marry. As high school seniors, over 80 percent of Millennials say that they think that they will marry, more than

---

[51] Decennial Census (1960); American Community Survey (2013).
[52] Isen and Stevenson (2010).
[53] Decennial Census (2000); American Community Survey (2010).

Generation Xers and Baby Boomers did at similar ages. Similarly, they are more likely to believe that they will have kids.

Figure 27: Percent Who Think They Will Marry and Have Kids

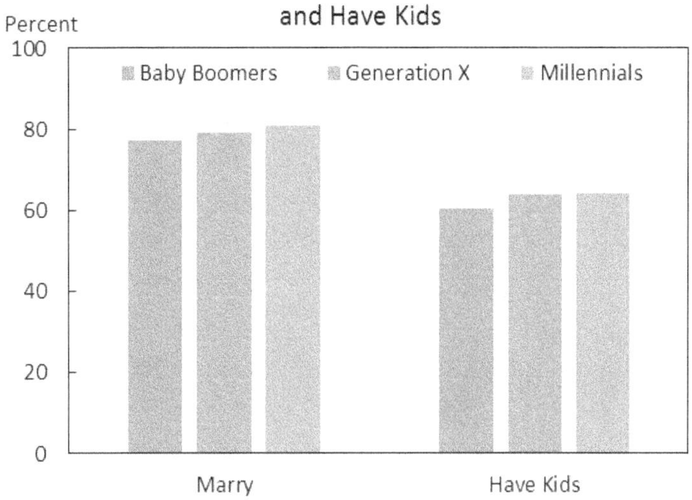

Source: Monitoring the Future, 1976-2011; CEA calculations.

Later marriage and longer time in school are also connected to delaying family formation until later in life. Figure 28 shows that age at first birth has risen considerably over time for women with advanced education, particularly for those with an advanced degree.

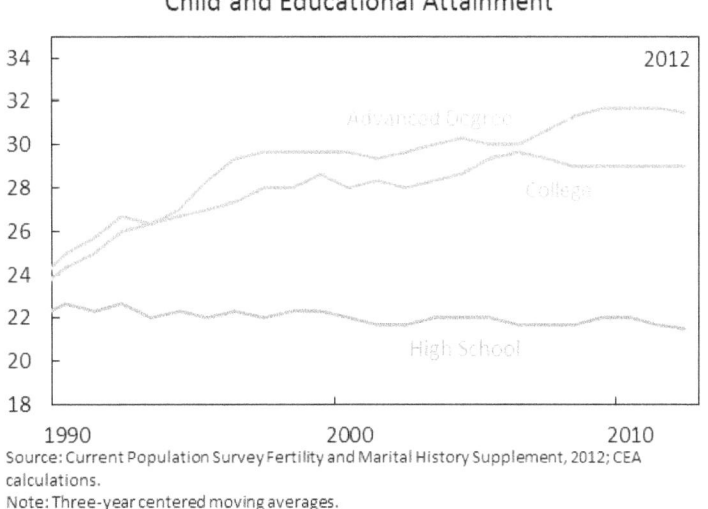

Figure 28: Median Age at First Birth by Birth Year of First Child and Educational Attainment

Source: Current Population Survey Fertility and Marital History Supplement, 2012; CEA calculations.
Note: Three-year centered moving averages.

Delayed family formation may also be a rational response in achieving both career and family aspirations. Most Millennials grew up in a household where all parents worked, and their children are even more likely to live in such a household. Accordingly, most Millennials will be working at the same time they are helping care for their families.

Balancing family and work obligations is difficult for many workers, particularly those who lack access to flexible work arrangements or paid leave.[54] While Millennials are more likely than older workers to have access to flexibility in where and when they work, only 45 percent have access to paid leave (compared to about 66 percent of older workers).[55] Millennials report that having a career and having a family is important, but at this stage, they may be focusing on establishing a career. Family formation may come once their careers are established, and they have higher earnings and are more likely to have access to workplace polices that help them balance work and family.

---

[54] CEA (2014b).
[55] American Time Use Survey (2011); CEA calculations.

Fact 14: Millennials are less likely to be homeowners than young adults in previous generations.

Entering adulthood during the Great Recession and recovery has not only affected Millennials' schooling and employment decisions, but also their housing and household formation patterns. In the aftermath of the Great Recession, the share of 18 to 34 year-olds living with their parents increased from 28 percent in 2007 to 31 percent in 2014 – which is a notable increase even if the actual magnitude falls well short of some popular perceptions. Correspondingly, the pace of household formation is low and the "headship rate" among Millennials – the rate at which Millennials head their own households – has fallen. With fewer Millennials as independent renters or homeowners, the demand for housing and the pace of residential investment is likely lower than the level implied by more typical rates of household formation and headship.

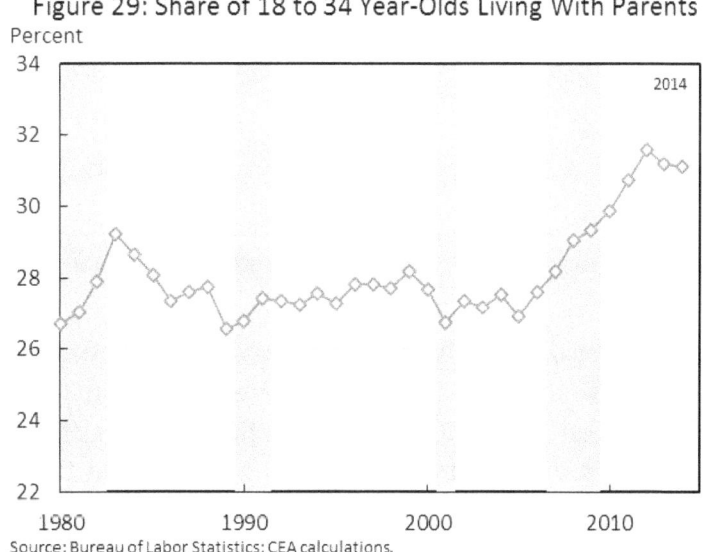

Figure 29: Share of 18 to 34 Year-Olds Living With Parents
Source: Bureau of Labor Statistics; CEA calculations.

As discussed in Fact 3, Millennials have stronger relationships with their parents than previous generations and parents of Millennials are much more involved in their children's lives. Perhaps it is not surprising that a generation that values living close to their families as much as Millennials would also be somewhat more likely to live with their parents as adults, particularly in an economy that is still recovering from a large recession.[56] Moreover, the increased enrollment of Millennials in college as discussed in Fact 4 may contribute to a rising share of Millennials living at home, as students often rely on their parents for housing and other financial support.[57]

---

[56] As shown in Fact 3, 49 percent of 12th grade Millennials said that living close to family and friends is very important to them, a 40 percent increase over what baby boomers said at that age. (Monitoring the Future, 1976-2011)

[57] Thompson (2014) and Fry (2014) argue that the increase in the share of young adults living at home with their parents stems from a classification issue, whereby those in college classify themselves in surveys as living at home. While these classification concerns are a contributing factor, we also find that even among 18 to 24 year-olds not enrolled in college and among 25 to 34 year-olds, the share living with their parents increased during the Great Recession and remains elevated.

The labor market is another factor contributing to the increased number of young adults living at home and the concurrent decline in headship. The rapid decline in the unemployment rate in recent years has somewhat boosted the headship rate and is putting downward pressure on the share living with their parents. Historically, the headship rate has had a significant cyclical component: since the 1970s, the headship rate among young adults has generally tracked their employment-to-population ratio closely.[58]

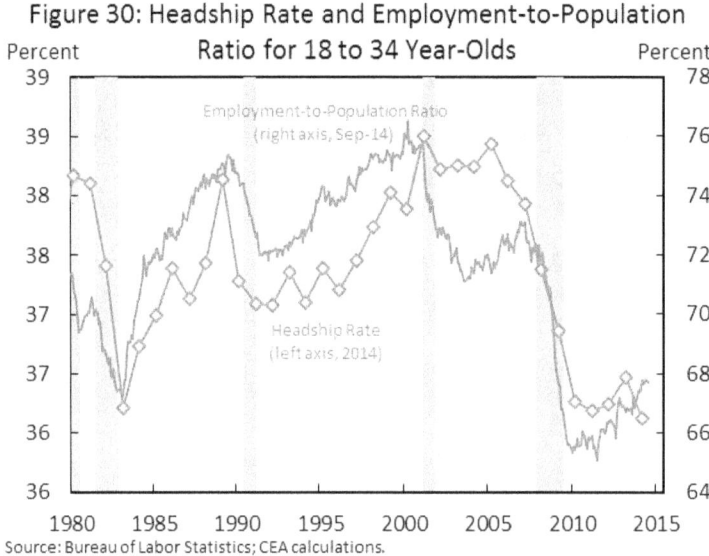

This cyclical relationship also holds at the state level: states with the largest increases in the unemployment rate relative to their averages before the Great Recession registered the largest declines in headship rates on average. With parents helping their children in times of labor market adversity, the majority of young adults living at home report that their own financial situation has improved.[59]

However, the share of Millennials living at home has increased even among those with jobs, which points to a role for factors outside the labor market. For instance, research suggests that increases in rents across many metropolitan areas during the Great Recession are likely to have depressed headship.[60] Moreover, the non-monetary costs of living at home may have decreased, again highlighting the role of the relationship between Millennials and their parents in explaining the former's housing choices. Today's parents report having fewer serious arguments with their children in their late teens than they had with their own parents at the same age. One in ten parents with children ages 16 to 24 say they "often" argue with their kids, while almost twice as many adults over

---

[58] Haurin et al. (1993); Whittington & Peters (1996); Ermisch & Salvo (1997); Ermisch (1999), Lee & Painter (2011); and Paciorek (2013).

[59] Parker (2012). The Boomerang Generation. Kaplan (2012) shows how the option to move back home provides insurance against adverse labor market outcomes, particularly among young adults that do not attend college.

[60] Paciorek (2013). More generally, higher housing costs bear a negative relationship with headship rates (see Haurin et al. (1993)).

30 report often having major arguments with their own parents.[61] Similarly, increased interaction with family does not appear to have a deleterious effect on the quality of Millennials' family ties. A recent survey found that Millennials living at home are just as satisfied with their family life as those who are not living at home.[62]

Consistent with lower headship rates, young adults today are less likely to be homeowners than young adults of previous generations. The decline in homeownership among Millennials, however, only looks particularly sharp when compared to the homeownership rates of 18 to 34 year-olds during the housing boom. Not surprisingly, the housing boom attracted a particularly large share of 18 to 34 year-olds relative to historical trends.

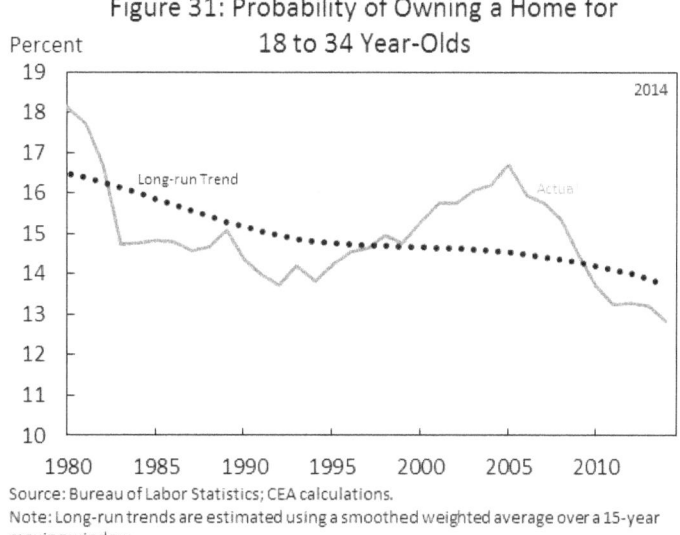

Taking a longer view, the lower likelihood of homeownership among Millennials today is largely in line with longstanding declines in homeownership among young people. While disentangling the factors contributing to contributing to the lower likelihood of owning a home in recent years is difficult, at least three forces appear to be at play. First, the gradual shifts in labor force participation, increased college enrollment, and delayed marriage discussed earlier in this report suggest that Millennials are delaying homeownership until they grow older, rather than substituting away from homeownership altogether. Millennials' stronger relationship with their parents and the accompanying reduction in headship reinforce this trend. It is likely for the Millennials living with their parents to first become renters before becoming homeowners, following the usual path to homeownership.

Second, the more recent decline in the probability of homeownership for 18 to 34 year-olds is strongly tied to the challenges in the labor market for Millennials due to the Great Recession that are discussed in Fact 9. However, homeownership decisions are often tied to job prospects and with the labor market

---

[61] Parker (2012).
[62] Ibid.

recovery well under way for Millennials, maintaining flexibility in their location decisions as renters could provide an advantage as they consider the job opportunities that come their way.

Lastly, today's tight lending environment may also be to blame. The share of those under age 30 with credit scores below 680 – a lower credit score on the spectrum from 300 to 850 – is approximately 67 percent, whereas this portion of the credit score distribution is less represented among older age groups. With regulatory constraints leading lenders to apply additional credit overlays for those with low credit scores, Millennials are likely to face challenges obtaining mortgage credit. Survey evidence collected by the Federal Reserve Bank of New York suggests that about 22 percent of borrowers with scores below 680 may decide not to apply for mortgage credit in the first place, perhaps because they feel discouraged by a prior rejected credit application, the lending environment, their employment prospects, or the financial burdens of paying down other debt.[63]

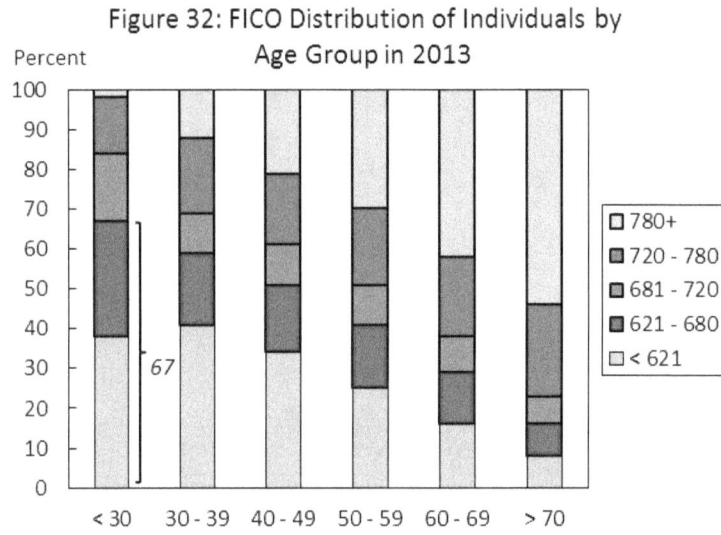

Figure 32: FICO Distribution of Individuals by Age Group in 2013
Source: Federal Reserve Bank of New York.

It is worth mentioning that some observers suggest that rising student loan debt burdens are dimming homeownership prospects for Millennials.[64] For many reasons, including the fact that their returns to education are still to be realized, it is too soon to draw firm conclusions about the long-lasting effects of the increase in aggregate student loan debt on homeownership. Several considerations suggest that the effect is likely to be concentrated in a small minority of Millennials who have student loan debt and are considering buying a home today. For one, because the presence of student loan debt generally "thickens" a credit record, providing more information about a person's payment history, and thus increases credit scores, the vast majority of those who are able to manage their payments and pay their loans on time preserve their access to credit, and many may even see their credit scores improve. Moreover, delinquencies on all types of credit have been steady in recent years, suggesting that, for some, the negative effect of missed student loan payments is somewhat offset by making consistent payments on their credit cards or auto loans.[65] Consistent with the fact that overall

---

[63] Zafar, Livingston, and van der Klaauw (2014).
[64] Brown, Caldwell, and Sutherland (2014). See Akers (2014) for an alternative view.
[65] Federal Reserve Bank of New York, Consumer Credit Panel (2014) and Dettling and Hsu (2014).

delinquencies have not been increasing in recent years, average credit scores among young adults have remained relatively constant. Lastly, research suggests that the extent to which higher student loan indebtedness is crowding out saving for a down payment appears to be modest so far, in part due to the higher returns to education facilitated by borrowing for college.

Fact 15: College-educated Millennials have moved into urban areas faster than their less educated peers.

Urban living in the United States has seen a resurgence during Millennials' lifetimes.[66] In keeping with this trend, Millennials are more likely to live in urban areas than earlier generations were at similar ages.[67] Growth in the share of 25 to 34 year-olds living in cities has been largest among mid-sized metropolitan areas (defined here as the 6th to 90th largest metro areas). These mid-size cities have attracted both college and non-college educated Millennials and have seen growth of around 5 percentage points in the share of the young adult population living in them today from 30 years ago. This is in keeping with long-term trends among the U.S. population generally, as the American population as a whole has moved from non-metropolitan areas towards mid-sized cities over the same 30-year period, albeit to a lesser extent.

The move toward cities has been greater among the college educated, who have increased their likelihood of living in both large and mid-sized cities. Overall, 73 percent of 25 to 34 year-olds with a college education were living in large or mid-sized cities in 2011, compared to 67 percent in 1980.[68] Among those without a college degree, 61 percent were living in large or mid-sized cities compared to 58 percent in 1980, and the growth in the share living in cities has only occurred in mid-sized cities.

Figure 33: Choice of Metropolitan Areas for 25 to 34 Year-Olds

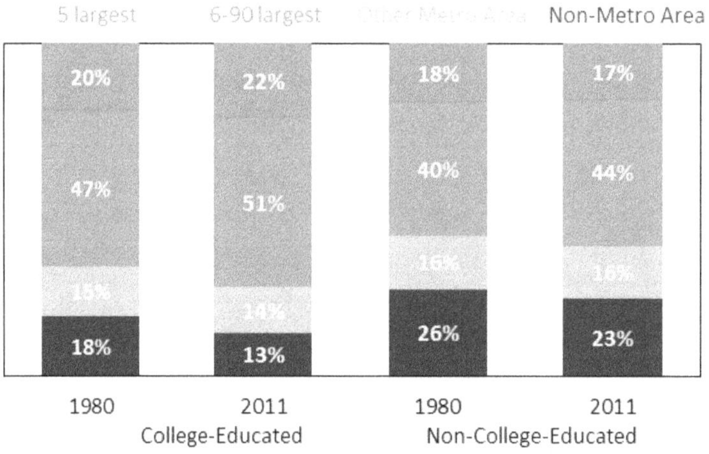

	1980	2011	1980	2011
	College-Educated		Non-College-Educated	
5 largest	20%	22%	18%	17%
6-90 largest	47%	51%	40%	44%
Other Metro Area	15%	14%	16%	16%
Non-Metro Area	18%	13%	26%	23%

Source: American Community Survey; CEA calculations.

College-educated Millennials are also somewhat more likely to live in a coastal city than their less-educated peers or Americans in general.[69] Americans overall are more likely to live in metropolitan

---

[66] Glaeser and Gottlieb (2006).
[67] Taylor and Keeter (2010).
[68] Changes to the coding of metro area residence in 2012 make it difficult to compare 1980 residence patterns with the most recent years of data.
[69] American Community Survey; CEA calculations.

areas away from the Atlantic or Pacific Coasts than they were in previous years. However, 25 to 34 year-olds in 2011 with a college education were slightly more likely to be found in a metropolitan area on the East or West Coast than they were around 30 years ago (33 percent versus 31 percent).[70] For those without a college degree, the proportion living on the coasts declined slightly over the same period (from 25 percent to 24 percent).[71]

Research in recent years has found that Americans with different levels of education are increasingly living in different areas. Berry and Glaeser (2005) note that since 1980, college graduates have gravitated towards urban areas that had higher levels of educational attainment at the beginning of this period, leading to increasing segregation by skill level across cities. Both Moretti (2013) and Diamond (2013) find that this geographic divergence has been partially driven by the demand for differently-skilled labor across cities. They also find that the divergence in skill levels across cities has been accompanied by diverging economic trajectories for "high-skilled" and "low-skilled" cities, suggesting that Millennials' increased sorting by skill has implications for economic opportunity.

---

[70] Ibid.
[71] Ibid.

Conclusion

The Millennial generation has taken part in many important transformations: from shifting ways of communicating and using technology, to changes in parenting practices, educational and career choices, and shifts in homeownership and family life. These developments have inspired much speculation about how this generation will fare later on in life and whether these trends are temporary or permanent. The answer to this question will depend, in part, on the policy choices we make in specific areas like education and housing and technology as well as the broader economic policies that help foster job creation and wage growth.

First, Millennials are a technologically connected, diverse, and tolerant generation. The priority that Millennials place on creativity and innovation augurs well for future economic growth, while their unprecedented enthusiasm for technology has the potential to bring change to traditional economic institutions as well as the labor market. For example, "crowdfunding" has enabled entrepreneurs to raise capital from diffuse sources online, rather than relying on traditional sources like banks to grow their businesses.[72]

Second, both Millennials' parents and Millennials themselves have made substantial investments in their human capital. Many of these trends are economically reasonable responses that will likely pay off for many Millennials over the long-term. For example, increasing college enrollment is a rational response to structural and cyclical trends: respectively, a labor market that confers ever large rewards on educated workers, and a weak job market which greatly reduced the opportunity cost of schooling during the downturn. Even as the economy improves, we expect enrollment to keep growing as long as college remains a worthwhile investment, albeit not as quickly as it had before. Moreover, Millennials are more likely than previous generations to study social science or applied fields that correspond to specific career paths.

Finally, as a result of the Affordable Care Act, Millennials are much more likely to have health insurance coverage than young workers in the past. Since the Affordable Care Act's dependent coverage provision went into effect in 2010, the uninsurance rate among Millennials has fallen by 13.2 percentage points. Increased health insurance coverage will likely translate into improved access to health care, health outcomes, and financial security. It may also have important labor market benefits: because the Affordable Care Act has made it easier for individuals to purchase their own health insurance, young adults are now better able to choose a job that fits their career goals, without having to worry about access to health insurance coverage.

That being said, challenges remain. First, research finds that macroeconomic conditions in childhood and young adulthood shape individuals' trajectories for years to come and can have lasting impacts on wages, earnings, savings and investment patterns, and trust in institutions among these individuals. This suggests that the Great Recession will at least affect Millennials' labor market performance as well as savings and investment behavior in the short-term, though at this point, it is still too soon to know how large and lasting these impacts will be.

---

[72] Hemer (2011); Agrawal, Catalini, and Goldfarb (2013).

Second, Millennials face a different labor market than previous generations, characterized by longer job tenure, fewer employer switches and career transitions, and lower overall fluidity. As a result, Millennials have stayed with their employers longer than Generation X workers did at the same point in their careers. At the moment however, the long-term impacts of these changes are unclear and there are both benefits and costs to longer tenure at jobs.

Third, total outstanding student loan debt has now surpassed $1 trillion in the second quarter of 2014, and there has been a recent increase in student debt delinquency rates even as delinquency rates on other types of debt have come down as the economy has recovered. In part, the growth of student loan debt is due to greater college enrollment among Millennials, but it is also due to a changing composition of students, rising tuition, reduced public funding, and diminished home equity. These trends raise concerns that some borrowers—particularly those who do not graduate from four-year institutions and those attending lower quality for-profit institutions—might face financial difficulties managing and paying down their debt. There are also concerns that students at these institutions might be receiving lower returns to their education.

Fourth, Millennials are less likely to own a home than previous generations. Homeownership trends have a significant cyclical component, as the household formation rate has historically closely tracked overall employment trends. The tight credit market has also made it more difficult to procure a mortgage. Nevertheless, longer-standing trends—liked getting married later—will continue to affect homeownership by this generation even after the economy has fully recovered.

Finally, in addition to these economic trends, Millennials are driving social and geographic shifts. Millennials are marrying later and less often than previous generations, while marriage rates have fallen especially sharply among the less-educated. In addition, Millennials—especially the more educated among them— have moved in large numbers to urban areas. These could have important economic implications for a long time to come because both marriage and geographic location have significant relationships with economic mobility and opportunity.[73]

So, while there are substantial challenges to meet, no generation has been better equipped to overcome them than Millennials. They are skilled with technology, determined, diverse, and more educated than any previous generation. Millennials are still in the early stages of joining and participating in the labor market. Taking steps to help them access and complete college, manage their student debt, have better opportunities for training and connection to jobs, access the credit they need for a home, protect the network neutrality that is the basis for much of their technological activity, as well as general policies to strengthen investment, job creation and wage growth, all have the potential to have a lasting impact for this generation and thus for U.S. economic performance for decades to come.

---

[73] Chetty, Hendren, Kline, and Saez (2014).

References

Agrawal, Ajay K., Christian Catalini, and Avi Goldfarb. 2013. "Some simple economics of crowdfunding." NBER Working Paper 19133.

Akers, Beth. 2014 "Reconsidering the Conventional Wisdom on Student Loan Debt and Home Ownership." The Brookings Institution.

Antwi, Yaa Akosa, Asako S. Moriya, and Kosali Simon. 2013. "Effects of Federal Policy to Insure Young Adults: Evidence from the 2010 Affordable Care Act's Dependent-Coverage Mandate." *American Economic Journal: Economic Policy*, 5(4): 1-28.

Antwi, Yaa Akosa, Asako S. Moriya, and Kosali Simon. 2014. "Access to Health Insurance and the Use of Inpatient Medical Care: Evidence from the Affordable Care Act Young Adult Mandate." NBER Working Paper 20202.

Baicker, Katherine and Amitabh Chandra. 2006. "The Labor Market Effects of Rising Health Insurance Premiums." Journal of Labor Economics 24, no. 3: 609-634.

Bailey, Martha J. and Susan M. Dynarski. 2011. "Inequality in Postsecondary Education." In G.J. Dunacan and R.J. Murnane (eds.), *Whither Opportunity? Rising Inequality, Schools, and Children's Life Chances.* New York, New York: Russell Sage.

Baum, Charles L. and Christopher J. Ruhm. 2014. "The Changing Benefits of Early Work Experience." NBER Working Paper 20413.

Berry, Christopher and Edward Glaeser. 2005. "The Divergence of Human Capital Levels Across Cities". NBER Working Paper 11617.

Blum, Alexander B., Lawrence C. Kleinman, Barbara Starfield, and Joseph S. Ross. 2012. "Impact of State Laws that Extend Eligibility for Parents' Health Insurance Coverage to Young Adults." *Pediatrics* 129(3): 426-432.

Brown, Meta, Sydnee Caldwell, and Sarah Sutherland. 2014. "Just Released: Young Student Loan Borrowers Remained on the Sidelines of the Housing Market in 2013." Liberty Street Economics. Federal Reserve Bank of New York.

Card, David. 1999. "The causal effect of education on earnings." Handbooks in Economics, 5 (3), 1801–1864.

Card, David and Thomas Lemieux. 2000. "Dropout and Enrollment Trends in the Post-War Period: What Went Wrong in the 1970s?" NBER Working Paper 7658.

Census Bureau. "America's Families and Living Arrangements: 2013: Adults," Table A1. http://www.census.gov/hhes/families/data/cps2013A.html.

Chetty, Raj, Nathaniel Hendren, Patrick Kline, and Emmanuel Saez. 2014. "Where is the Land of Opportunity? The Geography of Intergenerational Mobility in the United States." NBER Working Paper 19843.

Chua, Kao-Ping, and Benjamin D. Sommers. 2014. "Changes in Health and Medical Spending Among Young Adults Under Health Reform." *Journal of the American Medical Association.* 311(23): 2437-2439.

Congressional Budget Office (CBO). 2014. "Updated Estimates of the Effects of the Insurance Coverage Provisions of the Affordable Care Act, April 2014."

Cohen, Robin A. and Michael E. Martinez. 2014. "Health Insurance Coverage: Early Release of Estimates from the National Health Interview Survey, January-March 2014."

Council of Economic Advisers. 2014a. "Missed Opportunities: The Consequences of State Decisions Not to Expand Medicaid."

Council of Economic Advisers. 2014b. "Nine Facts About American Families and Work."

Davis, Steven J. and John Haltiwanger. 2014. "Labor Market Fluidity and Economic Performance." Prepared for the Federal Reserve Bank of Kansas City's symposium, August 21-23.

Deming, David J., Noam Yutchman, Amira Abulafi, Claudia Goldin, and Lawrence F. Katz. 2014. "The Value of Postsecondary Credentials in the Labor Market: An Experimental Study." NBER Working Paper 20528.

Depew, Briggs. 2013. "Expanded dependent health insurance coverage and the labor supply of young adults: Outcomes from state policies and the Affordable Care Act." Working Paper.

Dettling, Lisa and Joanne Hsu. 2014. "Returning to the Nest: Debt and Parental Co-residence Among Young Adults."

Devereux, Paul J. 2000. "Task Assignment over the Business Cycle." *Journal of Labor Economics*, 18 (1): 98-124.

Devereux, Paul J. 2002. "Occupational Upgrading and the Business Cycle." LABOUR, 16: 423–452.

Diamond, Rebecca. 2013. "The Determinants and Welfare Implications of U.S. Workers' Diverging Location Choices by Skill: 1980-2000." Harvard University, mimeograph. http://web.stanford.edu/~diamondr/jmp_final_121813.pdf.

Dillender, Marcus. 2014. "Do More Health Insurance Options Lead to Higher Wages? Evidence From States Extending Dependent Coverage." *Journal of Health Economics.* 36: 84-97.

Ermisch, John. 1999. "Prices, Parents, and Young People's Household Formation." *Journal of Urban Economics*. Elsevier, 45(1): 47-71.

Ermisch, John and Pamela Di Salvo. 1997. "The Economic Determinants of Young People's Household Formation." *Economica*. 64: 627–644.

Federal Reserve Bank of New York. 2014. "Quarterly Report on Household Debt and Credit." August 2014.

Fry, Richard. 2013a. "A Record 21.6 Million in 2012: A Rising Share of Young Adults Live in Their Parents' Home." Pew Research Center.

Fry, Richard. 2013b. "Millennials still lag in forming their own households." Pew Research Center.

Gellman, Lindsay. 2013. "Mom, Stop Calling, I'll Text You All Day." The Wall Street Journal.

Glaeser. Edward L. and Joshua D. Gottlieb. 2006. "Urban Resurgence and the Consumer City." Urban Studies 43(8): 1275-1299.

Goldin, Claudia, Lawrence Katz, and Ilyana Kuziemko. 2006. "The Homecoming of American College Women: The Reversal of the Gender Gap in College." *Journal of Economic Perspectives*, 20:133-156.

Goldman Sachs Research. 2014. "US Daily: Student Loan Debt: How Big a Problem?" https://360.gs.com/research/portal/research/econcommentary/?action=viewpage&st=1&d=17215026&portal.page.printable=true&isRouted=true.

Gruber, Jonathan and Alan B. Krueger. 1991. "The Incidence of Mandated Employer-Provided Insurance: Lessons From Workers' Compensation Insurance." In Tax Policy and the Economy, Volume 5, edited by David Bradford, pp. 111-144. Cambridge, MA: MIT Press.

Gruber, Jonathan. 1994. "The Incidence of Mandated Maternity Benefits." American Economic Review 84, no. 3: 622-641.

Haurin, Donald, Patric Hendershott and Dongwook Kim. 1993. "The Impact of Real Rents and Wages on Household Formation." *The Review of Economics and Statistics.* 75(2): 284-293.

Hemer, Joachim. 2011. "A snapshot on crowdfunding." No. R2/2011. Working papers firms and region.

Hoekstra, Mark. 2009. "The Effect of Attending the State Flagship University on Earnings: A Discontinuity-Based Approach." *The Review of Economics and Statistics.* 91(4): 717-724.

Howe, Neil, and William Strauss. 2000. "Millennials Rising: The Next Great Generation." New York. Vintage Books.

Hulbert, Jeffrey M. 2012. "The Impact of Dependent Coverage Legislation on the Job Choices of Young Adults."

Hyatt, Henry R. and James R. Spletzer. 2013. "The Recent Decline in Employment Dynamics." *IZA Journal of Labor Economics* 2(5).

Isen, Adam and Betsey Stevenson. 2010. "Women's Education and Family Behavior: Trends in Marriage, Divorce, and Fertility." NBER Working Paper 15725.

Kahn, Lisa B. 2010. "The Long-Term Labor Market Consequences of Graduating from College in a Bad Economy." *Labour Economics* 17: 303-316.

Kaplan, Greg. 2012. "Moving Back Home: Insurance Against Labor Market Risk". *Journal of Political Economy* 120(3): 446-512. Print.

Lee, Kwan-Ok and Gary Painter. 2011. "Housing Tenure Transitions of Older Households: How close do they want to live to their kids?" Lusk Center for Real Estate. University of Southern California.

Long, Bridget Terry. 2013. "The Financial Crisis and College Enrollment: How Have Students and Their Families Responded?" in *How the Great Recession Affected Higher Education*, eds. Jeffrey Brown and Caroline Hoxby.

Long, Sharon K., Genevieve M. Kenney, Stephen Zuckerman, Douglas Wissoker, Adele Shartzer, Michael Karpman, Nathaniel Anderson, and Katherine Hempstead. 2014. "Taking Stock at Mid-Year: Health Insurance Coverage Under the ACA as of June 2014."

Malmendier, Ulrike and Stefan Nagel. 2011. "Depression Babies: Do Macroeconomic Experiences Affect Risk-Taking?" *The Quarterly Journal of Economics* 126(1): 373-416.

Moretti, Enrico. 2013. "Real Wage Inequality." *American Economic Journal: Applied Economics* 5(1): 65-103.

National Center for Economic Statistics. 2012. National Post-Secondary Student Aid Study 2011-2012.

Oreopoulos, Philip, Till von Wachter, and Andrew Heisz. 2012. "Short- and Long-term Career Effects of Graduating in a Recession." *AEJ: Applied Economics*, 4(1): 1-29.

Paciorek, Andrew D. 2013. "The Long and the Short of Household Formation." Finance and Economics Discussion Series 2013-26. Board of Governors of the Federal Reserve System (U.S.).

Parker, Kim. 2012. "The Boomerang Generation." Pew Research Center.

Parker, Simon. 2009. *The Economics of Entrepreneurship* 114 (Cambridge).

Pew Research Center. 2014. "Parental Time Use." http://www.pewresearch.org/data-trend/society-and-demographics/parental-time-use/

Psacharopoulos, George and Harry Anthony Patrinos. 2004. "Returns to Investment in Education: A Further Update." *Education Economics* 12(2): 111-134.

Ramey, Garey and Valerie A. Ramey. 2010. "The Rug Rat Race." Brookings Papers on Economic Activity.

Saloner, Brendan, and Benjamin Lê Cook. 2014. "An ACA Provision Increased Treatment For Young Adults With Possible Mental Illnesses Relative To Comparison Group." *Health Affairs* 33(8): 1425-1434.

Scott-Clayton, Judith. "What explains trends in labor supply among US undergraduates, 1970-2009?" NBER Working Paper 17744.

Sisko, Andrea M., Sean P. Keehan, Gigi A. Cuckler, Andrew J. Madison, Sheila D. Smith, Christian J. Wolfe, Devin A. Stone, Joseph M. Lizonitz, and John A. Poisal. 2014. "National Health Expenditure Projections, 2013–23: Faster Growth Expected With Expanded Coverage And Improving Economy." Health Affairs 33(9):1-10.

Sommers, Benjamin D., Thomas Buchmueller, Sandra L. Decker, Colleen Carey, and Richard Kronick. 2013. "The Affordable Care Act has led to significant gains in health insurance and access to care for young adults." *Health Affairs* 32(1): 165-174.

Sommers, Benjamin D., Thomas Musco, Kenneth Finegold, Munira Z. Gunja, Amy Burke, and Audrey M. McDowell. 2014. "Health Reform and Changes in Health Insurance Coverage in 2014." New England Journal of Medicine 371, no. 9: 867-874.

Summers, Lawrence H. 1989. "Some Simple Economics of Mandated Benefits." The American Economic Review 79, no. 2: 177-183.

Taylor, Paul and Scott Keeter. 2010. "Millennials: Confident. Connected. Open to Change." Pew Research Center.

Thompson, Derek. 2014. "The Misguided Freakout About Basement-Dwelling Millennials." The Atlantic.

Topel, Robert H. and Michael P. Ward. 1992. "Job Mobility and the Careers of Young Men." *Quarterly Journal of Economics* 107(2): 439-479.

United States Department of the Treasury. 2014. "Remarks of Deputy Secretary Raskin at the Annual meeting of the National Association for Business Economics." http://www.treasury.gov/press-center/press-releases/Pages/jl2652.aspx

Waldfogel, Joel. 2013. "Digitization and the Quality of New Media Products: The Case of Music." In *Economics of Digitization,* eds. Avi Goldfarb, Shane Greenstein, and Catherine Tucker.

Whittington, Leslie and H. Elizabeth Peters. 1996. "Economic Incentives for Financial and Residential Independence." *Demography*. 33(1): 82–97.

Wozniak, Abigail. 2010. "Are College Graduates More Responsive to Distant Labor Market Opportunities?" 2010. *Journal of Human Resources*. 45(4): 944-970. Revised version of "Educational Differences in the Migration Response of Young Workers to Local Labor Market Conditions," *IZA Discussion Paper* #1954.

Young Invincibles. 2011. "New Polls Finds More than Half of Millennials Want to Start Businesses." http://www.kauffman.org/~/media/kauffman_org/research%20reports%20and%20covers/2011/11/millennials_study.pdf

Zafar, Basit, Max Livingston, and Wilbert van der Klaauw. 2014. "Rising Household Debt: Increasing Demand or Increasing Supply?" Liberty Street Economics. Federal Reserve Bank of New York.

Zimmerman, Seth D. 2014. "The Returns to Four-Year College for Academically Marginal Students." *Journal of Labor Economics*. 32(4).

www.ingramcontent.com/pod-product-compliance
Lightning Source LLC
Chambersburg PA
CBHW080606190526
45169CB00007B/2896